JANE EYRE

Charlotte Brontë

Abridged and adapted by S. E. Paces

A PACEMAKER CLASSIC

Fearon Education
a division of
David S. Lake Publishers
Belmont, California

Other Pacemaker Classics

The Adventures of Tom Sawyer
The Deerslayer
Dr. Jekyll and Mr. Hyde
Frankenstein
Great Expectations
The Jungle Book
The Last of the Mohicans
The Moonstone
Robinson Crusoe
A Tale of Two Cities
The Three Musketeers
The Time Machine
Treasure Island
20,000 Leagues Under the Sea
Two Years Before the Mast

Library of Congress Catalog Card Number: 86-81660

ISBN 0-8224-9286-5

Printed in the United States of America

1. 9 8 7 6 5 4 3 2

Contents

1 The Red Room

That afternoon we didn't go out. We didn't take a walk as we usually did. We stayed at home because the weather was rainy, windy, and cold.

We sat in the living room. My aunt, Mrs. Reed, had her children around her. Eliza, Georgiana, and John sat near their mother, who was resting on a couch. I sat alone. They didn't want me near them.

My aunt had never liked me. She let me live with her, but she was always unkind to me. Her children—my cousins—were cruel to me. They didn't want me at Gateshead, which is what their house was called. I was a poor orphan, only ten years old. I had no friends. Nobody wanted me.

I went into the next room. Here there was a bookcase full of interesting books. I chose a book that was full of pictures. I then sat behind the curtains in the window seat. I began to read. Reading made me forget my troubles.

Suddenly I heard a shout, "Where is she?" It was my cousin John's voice. John was four years older than I. Every day he used to hit me. He was the meanest of all my cousins.

Then I heard Eliza say, "She's hiding behind that curtain."

"Come out! If you don't come out, I'll pull you out!" said John.

I came out, trembling with fear. "He'll hit me again," I was thinking.

John hit me hard, and then he said, "What were you doing behind that curtain?"

"I was reading."

"Show me the book!"

Silently I handed the book to him.

"I'm the master here," John said, "and I forbid you to take our books! You eat our food, you sleep in our house, and now you're taking our books! Nobody wants you here. You should be in the streets." His face was red with anger. "Go and stand by the door!" he shouted.

I obeyed him. He lifted his arm and threw the heavy book at my head. It hit me and I fell to the floor, striking my head against the door. My head began to bleed. It hurt me very much. I got up and rushed at John. "You wicked, cruel boy!" I shouted.

He hit me again. I fought him like a wildcat. I scratched and I bit him. "You rat! You rat!" he screamed. I was wild with pain and anger.

Two servants rushed in. Mrs. Reed followed them.

"What a wicked child she is!" said one of the servents. "She was trying to kill our young master!"

"Take her to the Red Room. Lock her in there!" Mrs. Reed commanded.

The servants carried me into the Red Room. They put me in a chair. "If you don't sit quietly, we'll tie you to the chair," one of them said. I was afraid, and I sat quite still.

Bessie, the nicer of the two servants, said, "You shouldn't hit your cousins. Your aunt is good to you. If she didn't keep you here, who would look after you? You ought to be thankful to your aunt."

They went out after that. I heard the key turn in the lock. I was locked in the Red Room!

The Red Room had always frightened me. My uncle had died there. After his death nobody went inside that room. I was afraid because I feared his ghost.

The room grew darker. It was evening now. Night would come soon—and I had no candle. I could hear the wind and the rain outside. I began to feel cold. My heart was heavy. My fears grew in the darkness. Suddenly I saw a light. "The ghost! It is the ghost!" I thought. I screamed then.

The servants came running. They unlocked the door in a great hurry. "What is the matter, Miss Eyre? Are you ill?" asked Bessie.

"Oh! Let me out, Bessie," I begged. I took her hand and held it fast. "Let me out!" I cried. "There's a ghost in here. Bessie, I'm afraid."

"What's the matter with her?" said Mrs. Reed, who had also come in.

"She's afraid," answered Bessie.

"Afraid! Oh, no! She's not afraid. She's only pretending." She turned to me and said, "You will stay here an hour longer."

"Oh, Aunt! Have pity! Forgive me! Don't make me stay here! Please! Please!"

"Be quiet!" She turned to the servants and said, "Lock her in!"

They locked me in again. When they had gone, I grew more and more afraid. The fear and the pain were too much for me. I fell to the floor, senseless.

When my senses came back to me, I found myself in my own bed. A bright fire was burning in the room, and a candle was burning on the table beside my bed. Oh, how glad I was! How thankful I was for the warmth and the light! I heard soft voices, too. Then I saw Bessie, who was sitting at the foot of my bed. Besides Bessie, there was the doctor. He was sitting in a chair beside my bed. He spoke to me softly and kindly.

"Well . . . do you know me?" he asked.

"Yes," I answered weakly.

He smiled at me and said, "You'll soon be better." To Bessie he said, "Let her sleep now. I'll come to see her in the morning." He picked up his bag and left.

"Do you want anything to eat or drink?" Bessie asked me kindly.

"No, thank you, Bessie."

"Then I'll go to bed. Call me if you want anything," Bessie said. I couldn't sleep but I lay there quietly. I felt very troubled and unhappy. My head—as well as my heart—was full of pain.

The next morning the doctor came again. "How is she?" he asked Bessie.

"She's better this morning," answered Bessie.

"She looks very sad," said the doctor, and he asked me, "Have you any pain?"

"No, sir."

"But you have been crying."

I couldn't answer him. I wanted to cry again.

At that moment a loud bell rang. It was the bell for the servants' dinner. Bessie had to leave us. When we were alone the doctor asked me, "Tell me, my child, what made you ill?"

"They locked me in a room where there was a ghost!"

"A ghost! But there aren't any ghosts!"

"Oh, yes! Mr. Reed's ghost was in the room. I saw it! And I was locked in—without a candle!"

"And what has made you sad this morning?"

"I have no father or mother, and no brothers or sisters."

"But you have a kind aunt. And you have kind cousins."

"Kind! They aren't kind! They're nasty and cruel. John hit me. He hits me every day. And my aunt locked me in the Red Room."

"Then you don't like living here?"

"I hate it!"

"Have you any other relatives?"

"I don't know."

"Would you like to go to school?"

I didn't know what school was, but I thought, "School can't be worse than Gateshead. It may be better." After a time I said, "Yes, I should like to go to school."

"Perhaps I can help you," said the doctor.

That evening Bessie said to me, "Mrs. Reed is going to send you to school very soon."

A month later a visitor arrived at Gateshead. I was making my bed when the doorbell rang loudly. Bessie came in and said to me, "Your aunt wants you in the living room at once." She brushed my hair hurriedly, and I went slowly downstairs.

I hadn't seen Mrs. Reed since the night in the Red Room. I was afraid. "Why does she want to see me? Who has come?" I asked myself. I opened the living room door.

Mrs. Reed was seated at her usual place by the fire. Beside her a tall man was standing. He was dressed in black. I stood in the doorway till Mrs. Reed called, "Come forward, Jane Eyre!" I went toward them.

"This is the child," said Mrs. Reed to the man in black.

"How old is she?" he asked in a deep voice.

"Ten."

"She's very small." He turned to me and asked, "Are you a good child?"

I didn't answer.

Mrs. Reed answered for me, "She's a wicked little girl, Mr. Brocklehurst. She tells lies. When she comes to your school, you must watch her carefully. She must learn to work hard. She is poor. When she grows up, she will have to earn her living by hard work."

Mr. Brocklehurst nodded his head in agreement. "I quite understand," he said.

Mr. Brocklehurst didn't stay long. After he had gone, I sat there quietly. I was watching Mrs. Reed, who was sewing. My heart was filled with anger and hatred for her. My eyes showed my feelings. She looked up from her sewing and said, "Leave the room at once!"

I got up obediently and moved toward the door. Then I turned back. I went up to her and said, "I'm not wicked. And I don't tell lies!" I was trembling with anger while I spoke. I could hardly breathe, but I went on, "People may think you are a good woman, but you're not! You're wicked and cruel!"

Mrs. Reed looked frightened. "What is the matter with you, Jane? Would you like to drink some water?"

"No, thank you, Mrs. Reed."

"Then go and lie down, my dear, or you will be ill again."

"I'm not your 'dear.' Send me to school, Mrs. Reed. I hate you! I hate living here!"

Mrs. Reed picked up her sewing and left the room quickly.

2 Lowood School

A few days later I left Gateshead for Lowood School. I left at six o'clock on a cold, damp morning. Bessie walked with me to the coach. She kissed me. "Be a good girl," she said. "Look after her!" she called to the driver.

I don't remember much about the journey. It seemed endless to me. We passed through several towns. We stopped at a large one. The driver took his horses to a stable. The passengers went into the inn for dinner. I sat alone in the big dining room. I had eaten no breakfast, and I could eat no dinner. I was tired and sad and afraid. "What is going to happen to me in Lowood School?" I asked myself.

We continued our journey. It became dark. I fell asleep. I was sleeping when the coach suddenly stopped and woke me up.

"Is there a little girl named Jane Eyre here?" a voice asked.

The driver answered, "Yes," and I got out of the coach. My trunk was taken out. The coach drove away. I stood there in the darkness, the wind, and the rain.

"Come this way," the voice said. I followed a woman up a wide path to a big building. There were lights in many windows. The woman led me through a long passage to a room with a bright fire in it. She left me there alone.

I hurried toward the fire because I was feeling very cold. A tall woman came in. Another woman was close behind her. The tall woman said kindly to me, "Are you tired, my child?"

"A little, ma'am."

"And hungry too, I'm sure." She turned to the other woman and said, "Miss Miller, let her have some supper before she goes to bed."

"Is this the first time that you have left home?" she asked me.

"I have no home. I have no parents. My mother and my father are both dead."

The tall woman, who was the headmistress, asked me other questions. "How old are you?" "Can you read?" "Do you know how to sew?" "Have you learned how to write?"

After I had answered all her questions, the headmistress, whose name was Miss Temple, left us. Miss Miller then led me to the classroom. There were many girls in the classroom. They were doing their homework.

"Monitors!" cried Miss Miller. "Collect the books and put them away!" The monitors obeyed. "Monitors! Fetch the supper trays!" The monitors went

out. Soon they came back. Each monitor was carrying a tray with a plate of bread, a jug of water, and a cup. I drank a little water, but I couldn't eat anything. I was too tired to eat.

After supper the girls went up to the dormitory. They undressed quickly and got into bed. Miss Miller helped me to undress because I was so tired. The lights were put out and I fell asleep at once.

The next morning a loud bell awakened me before dawn. I rose and dressed with the other girls. We all shivered because the dormitory was icy cold. The bell rang again. Two by two, we went downstairs to the classroom.

At first there was a lot of noise. Miss Miller had to shout again and again, "Silence!" "Stop talking!" "Be quiet!" At last the girls sat down in different groups. Each group sat in a half-circle in front of a teacher's table. I was put in the lowest class. I was so glad when the breakfast bell rang. I felt ill from hunger. I had eaten nothing the day before.

We went into the dining room and sat down in our places. There was hot porridge in the bowls on the table. It smelled bad because the porridge was burnt. I took a spoonful and then put down my spoon quickly. Although I was very hungry, I couldn't eat that burnt porridge. It tasted so bad nobody could eat it.

"It's burnt again!" the girls said. They were all angry. They were all so hungry!

We went back to our classes. There was only one classroom, and all the classes were held in that room at the same time. Our lessons began. Different classes had different lessons: geography, history, grammar, writing, arithmetic, and music.

When the clock was striking twelve, the headmistress came in. "I have something to say to the girls," she said. "This morning you were given a breakfast that you couldn't eat. You are hungry. Therefore I have ordered some bread and cheese for all of you." The bread and cheese were brought in. Oh, how good it tasted!

After that an order was given, "Out, into the garden!" We all went outside. The garden was a sad place on that January day. The weather was cold and damp. The trees were leafless. There were no flowers.

Nobody played with me. No one spoke to me. I stood there alone. That didn't trouble me much. I was used to loneliness. I looked at the words above the door of the school: Lowood Institution. "What is the meaning of the word 'Institution'?" I asked myself.

Then I heard a cough. I turned my head. I saw a girl sitting on a stone bench. Her head was bent over a book. She was reading. When she looked up I asked her, "Can you tell me the meaning of those words?" I pointed to the words "Lowood Institution."

"That's the name of our school. It's a school for orphans and poor children."

"Do we pay any money? Do they keep us here for nothing?"

"We pay very little."

At that moment the bell rang. It stopped my questions. We all went inside for dinner.

Dinner was nearly as bad as breakfast. Nearly, but not quite! They gave us tough meat and almost rotten potatoes. I ate what I could, which was very little!

After dinner there were more lessons. Then we had to do our homework. We were given some bread and water before we went to bed. That was the end of my first day at Lowood School.

The next day we got up before sunrise. We couldn't wash because the water was frozen in our jugs. The air was icy. When breakfast time came, I felt ill from hunger and cold. The porridge wasn't burnt this time. But how little they gave us!

I found the lessons long and difficult. Many things were new to me. I felt tired and troubled. I was glad when the teacher asked me to sew. I sat there quietly.

While I was sewing, I listened to the history lesson. My friend of the day before was answering the teacher's questions. She was answering them cleverly. But the teacher, Miss Scatcherd, didn't praise her. Instead she said angrily, "Burns, you didn't wash your hands this morning!" The girl didn't say a word. Why didn't she say, "The water was frozen, and we couldn't wash"? She kept silent.

"Fetch me the cane!" Miss Scatcherd said. The girl obediently fetched the cane. The teacher struck her a dozen times with the cane. The girl didn't cry. She didn't make a sound. She just stood there quietly.

That evening, at playtime, I went up to her. I asked her, "What is your name, besides Burns?"

"Helen."

"Do you come from far away?"

"Oh, yes! I come from the North, near Scotland."

"Don't you wish to go away from here?"

"No. Why should I?" She added, "They sent me here to learn. I must learn!"

"But Miss Scatcherd is so cruel to you—"

"Cruel? Oh, no! She's strict. She dislikes my faults. And I have so many faults!"

"If she struck me, I should strike her back!"

"If you did that, Mr. Brocklehurst would send you away. What would happen then?"

"You say you have many faults, Helen. I can't believe you. I think that you are very, very good."

"Oh, no! I'm not. I'm careless and I'm untidy. I ought to obey the rules, but I don't. Instead of learning my lessons, I am always reading."

"Is Miss Temple as unkind as Miss Scatcherd?"

Helen smiled and answered, "Oh, no! Miss Temple is different from Miss Scatcherd. Miss Temple is so good and so kind! She tells me when I am doing wrong. But she tells me gently. And when I'm doing right, she praises me."

"If I were you, I should hate Miss Scatcherd!"

"Oh, no! We must try to love those who are unkind to us. We must try to love our enemies."

"Then I ought to love Mrs. Reed and her son John! That is quite impossible. I hate them! I shall always hate them!"

"Tell me about them," said Helen.

I told her about my life at Gateshead. When I had finished, I asked her, "Don't you think that Mrs. Reed is a wicked, cruel woman?"

"She was unkind to you, that is true. But you must try to forgive her. If you try to do that, you will be happier. Life is so short. We must be happy while we can. Life is so short," Helen repeated sadly, and fell silent.

A monitor came up to us then. "Helen Burns, if you don't go and tidy your drawer, I shall tell Miss Scatcherd!" she said.

Helen got up and obeyed at once.

3 "This Girl Is a Liar!"

One afternoon, while we were having an arithmetic lesson, Mr. Brocklehurst came in. All the girls, and the teachers, too, stood up. I was afraid when I saw him. He was talking to Miss Temple. Was he talking about me? I hid my face behind my book. "I hope he doesn't see me!" I said to myself.

Suddenly I dropped my book. It fell with a loud crash. Everybody turned and looked at me.

"Careless girl!" exclaimed Mr. Brocklehurst. He looked at me. "Ah!" he said, "I know that child. She is the new pupil. I have something to say about her. Come here!" he ordered. My legs shook under me. I could hardly walk. Two girls pushed me toward Mr. Brocklehurst.

"Stand on that chair!" I climbed up onto a high chair. There I stood, in front of the whole school.

"This girl is a *liar!*" said Mr. Brocklehurst. "Her kind aunt has told me about her. She is a wicked, thankless, shameful child!" To Miss Temple he said, "Let her stand there for half an hour. Let no one speak to her for the rest of the day!"

I cannot tell you how I felt! I was filled with shame and anger and sadness. I wished to die!

When the bell rang, the girls went into the dining room for tea. I climbed down from the high chair. I crept into a corner and wept like a lost child.

Helen Burns came to me. She brought me my tea and bread. "Come, try and eat something," she said gently. I tried but I couldn't eat anything. I went on crying. Helen sat down beside me.

"Why," I asked her, "are you sitting here with a girl—who is a liar?"

"We're all sorry for you, Jane."

"Sorry for me—when Mr. Brocklehurst says I am a liar?"

"Nobody here likes Mr. Brocklehurst. The girls are your friends—and the teachers as well. Besides, Jane, what does it matter? If you know you are not a liar, then all is well. Let people say what they like! You need not be ashamed."

A week later Miss Temple told the whole school that I was no liar. I had told her all about my life at Gateshead. Miss Temple said she knew the doctor there and would write a letter to him asking about me. She received an answer from the doctor. He had spoken very well of me. All the school was very pleased and I, of course, was very happy.

I began to study hard. My work improved. Soon I was moved to a higher class. My teachers praised me. Life was hard and uncomfortable at Lowood, but by now I had become used to it. And I felt lucky to have two wonderful friends—Helen and Miss Temple.

The winter passed and the spring came. The sun was warm. The garden was green and bright with flowers of all colors. On Thursday afternoons we had a half-holiday. We went for walks in the valley in which the school stood.

In May many girls fell ill with fever. The illness spread quickly. Nearly everyone became ill. Some girls died. The rest of us did what we liked. We had no lessons. The school was like a hospital now. The teachers had to be nurses.

Helen was also ill. But her illness was not the fever that the other girls had. Her lungs were very weak. She was staying in Miss Temple's room, and the nurse allowed nobody to see her. One evening the doctor came very late. That was unusual. "Somebody is going to die," I thought. I asked the nurse, "How is Helen Burns?"

"Very weak," she answered.

"What does the doctor say?"

"She can't last long."

That night, when everyone was in bed, I crept to Miss Temple's room. Miss Temple was not there. The nurse was there but she was asleep. I crept toward Helen's bed.

"Helen!" I whispered. "It's Jane. Are you awake, Helen?"

"Jane!" she exclaimed in a weak voice. "Why have you come? It's so late!"

"They told me you were very ill. I had to come to see you. I wanted to speak to you."

"You've come to say 'good-bye,' Jane."

"Are you going home then, Helen?"

"Yes, Jane. I'm going home. I'm going to my last home."

"No! No! Helen—"

Helen began to cough. She couldn't speak. She could hardly breathe. At last she was able to say, "I'm going to God, Jane. And I'm happy. You must be happy, too. When I'm dead, don't be sad! Be happy, Jane!"

She began coughing again. At last she said, "I feel so tired! I shall sleep now. Don't leave me, Jane! Stay here with me!"

"I'll stay with you, dear Helen." I lay down beside her. She kissed me. Soon we were both asleep. When I awoke, it was morning, but Helen had "gone home." Helen was dead.

4 I Become a Teacher

The fever caused the death of many girls. However, it had one good result. Public attention was drawn to the school. Many improvements followed. A new school was built. The new building was bigger and more healthful than the old one. Our food was improved, and our clothing also. The school became a tolerable place.

I stayed at Lowood eight years. During the last two years I was a teacher there. I enjoyed my work. Helen had "gone home" but Miss Temple remained my dear true friend. Then Miss Temple got married and left the school. She went to live far away.

Without Miss Temple my life seemed empty. I suddenly felt that I, too, must leave the school. I wanted to go out into the wide world. I wanted to see new places. I wanted to live among other people. I decided to put this advertisement in the newspaper:

A young lady-teacher is looking for work in a private family, where the children are under fourteen. She is able to teach the usual school subjects, as well as French, drawing, and music. Address: J. E., The Post Office, Lowton.

Lowton was the name of a nearby town where I mailed my letter to the newspaper. A week later I went to the Lowton post office. There was a letter for me. I opened the letter, and I read :

If J. E. is able to send a good report of her character, I can offer her work. She will have to teach a little girl who is seven years old. She will receive thirty pounds a year. Address: Mrs. Fairfax, Thornfield Hall, Millcote.

I read that letter many times. In the end I knew it by heart! The next morning I told the head-mistress about my plan. She gave me the necessary report. I sent this at once to Mrs. Fairfax.

Very soon I received the answer. Mrs. Fairfax was satisfied with the report. She asked me to come to Thornfield Hall at once.

The journey by coach to Millcote was a long one. I left Lowton at four o'clock in the morning. I arrived at Millcote at eight o'clock in the evening. A carriage was waiting for me there. After a two-hour drive we reached Thornfield Hall.

A servant opened the door. "Will you come this way, please, ma'am?" she asked. I followed the servant down a long passage to a small but comfortable room.

A bright fire was burning. Beside it sat an old lady in a black silk dress and a white apron. She got up and came toward me. She welcomed me with a smile and introduced herself as Mrs. Fairfax.

"Come to the fire, my dear," she said very kindly. "You must be so cold after your long journey. Sit down here." She made me sit in her own comfortable armchair. "You need a hot drink, I'm sure," she said. "I'll go and fetch it, and I shall tell John to carry your trunk up to your room."

When she came back she said, "I'm so glad you're here. I feel lonely sometimes. Now I can talk to you." She looked at the clock. "Why, it's already past midnight. You must be very tired. Come with me! I'll show you to your room."

Mrs. Fairfax took a candle and led the way upstairs. We walked along a long passage and stopped at a room at the end.

"Good night, my dear," she said in a very kind voice.

I slept well that night. When I awoke, the room was filled with sunshine. It was a pretty room, much prettier than the one I had in Lowood. I felt hopeful. A new life was in front of me!

I got up, washed, and dressed myself. Then I went outside and wandered around the grounds. I saw that the house was quite large. It had three floors and there was a very big garden. Mrs. Fairfax came out to join me.

"You're an early riser," she said. "What do you think of Thornfield?"

"It's beautiful—and so big! I like it very much."

"Yes, it's a nice place," she agreed. "But it's in need of repair. It's a pity that Mr. Rochester comes here so seldom."

"Mr. Rochester? Who is he?"

"He's the owner of Thornfield."

"Doesn't it belong to you?"

She laughed, and then she explained, "I'm only the housekeeper."

"And who is the little girl, my pupil?"

"Adele Varens. Mr. Rochester is her guardian."

At that moment a little girl came running toward us. Her nurse was close behind her.

"Adele!" said Mrs. Fairfax, "Say 'good morning' to this lady. She is going to teach you."

"Is she my governess?" Adele asked her nurse. She spoke in French and the nurse answered her in the same language.

"Are they French?" I asked Mrs. Fairfax.

"The nurse is. Adele was born in Paris. She left Paris only six months ago. When she first came here, she couldn't speak a word of English. Now she can speak a little."

After breakfast I went with Adele to the library. We began our lessons. Adele was quite a clever little girl, but she was restless. At about midday our lessons ended. I went to look for Mrs. Fairfax. I found her working in the dining room.

"What sort of man is Mr. Rochester?" I asked.

"Well . . . he's rather a strange man. He has traveled a lot. He has seen a great deal of the world. He doesn't come to Thornfield very often. When he comes, he never stays long. Would you like to see the rest of the house?" she asked me.

She took me downstairs, and then upstairs. After Lowood the house seemed like a palace! At last she said, "And now, I must show you the view from the roof."

The view was wonderful. There were fields, woods, hills, the village, the church, and a long white road.

We came down from the roof. I went first. Mrs. Fairfax stayed behind to lock the door to the roof. I waited for her in the long passage on the top floor. This passage was narrow and rather dark because it had only one small window.

While I was waiting there, a strange thing happened. I heard a loud laugh. It stopped. Then it began again. It grew louder and louder. It was a strange laugh, not a happy laugh. It didn't even sound like a human laugh! I felt afraid.

"Mrs. Fairfax!" I called. "Are you there?"

"I'm coming," she said, and I heard her coming down the stairs.

"Did you hear that laugh?" I asked her. "Who was it? What was it?"

"Oh! . . . One of the servants . . . Grace Poole, I think. She comes up here to do her sewing." Then she called, "Grace!"

A door close to me opened, and a servant came out. She was an unusually strong-looking woman, about forty years old, and her face was hard.

"There's too much noise, Grace! You must be quiet. Remember what the master has said!"

"Yes, ma'am," the woman said obediently.

5 The Master of Thornfield Hall

Life at Thornfield Hall was very pleasant. Mrs. Fairfax was always kind and friendly. Adele was a nice little girl, although she was rather spoiled. I liked teaching her. The days passed peacefully and happily.

One afternoon in January, I went out for a walk to the next village to mail a letter. It was a cold winter day. The ground was frozen, and there was a lot of ice on the road. There was a deep silence over the hills and the woods.

Then the silence was broken. I heard the sound of a horse. It was coming nearer. A big dog rushed by. The horse followed. Suddenly the horse and its rider fell down on the icy road! I ran toward the traveler, who was trying to get up.

"Are you hurt, sir?" I asked.

He didn't answer me.

"Can I help you?"

"Stand over there," he said roughly. I obeyed. At last he was able to stand up. He helped his horse to stand. Then he sat down at the side of the road. He seemed to be in great pain.

"If you need help, sir, I can fetch somebody from Thornfield Hall."

I looked at the traveler's face. It wasn't the face of a young man. He was about forty years old. He looked troubled and angry. "I'm all right," he said sharply. "Please leave me alone."

"How can I leave you here alone? It's so late. Can you get on your horse?" I asked him.

He looked at me for the first time. "Who are you?" he asked. "Where do you come from?"

"From Thornfield Hall."

"But who are you? You're not a servant."

"I'm the governess."

"Ah!" he said. "I remember now."

He got up. Slowly and painfully he tried to walk toward his horse, but he could not.

"I must ask you to help me," he said. "Come here!"

I went near him. He laid a heavy hand on my shoulder. We walked to the horse. With a great effort he was able to get on its back.

In a moment, the horse, its rider, and the dog had all disappeared.

When I got back to Thornfield later that evening, I went to Mrs. Fairfax's room. She wasn't there. A great dog lay in front of the fire. I needed a candle and so I rang the bell. When the servant came in, I asked her, "Whose dog is this?"

"It's the master's, Mr. Rochester's."

"Mr. Rochester's!"

"Yes. The master has just arrived. Mrs. Fairfax is with him. Miss Adele is there, too. John has gone for the doctor. The master has had an accident. His horse fell on the icy road. The master has hurt his leg badly."

I saw little of Mr. Rochester for several days. In the mornings he was busy. In the evenings some gentlemen who lived nearby came to visit him.

One evening, he asked Mrs. Fairfax, Adele, and me to come to the dining room. Adele was excited. "He's going to give me my presents, Miss Eyre!" she said. When we entered the dining room, we saw a large box on the table. "My presents!" exclaimed Adele, and she ran toward the table.

"Yes, take your presents, Adele!" said Mr. Rochester. "Sit down in that corner with Mrs. Fairfax, and be quiet!"

"Come here, Miss Eyre," he said to me. "Take this chair." He pointed to a chair near his own armchair. He was smiling. He was silent for some minutes, looking at the fire. While he was doing that, I looked at his face. "What kind of man is he?" I asked myself.

Suddenly he asked me, "Well . . . do you think me handsome?"

"No, sir," I answered.

"Ah! Then my face doesn't please you?"

"Excuse me, sir, I spoke too freely."

"No. Tell me what you think! Do you think I am a foolish man?"

"Oh, no, sir!" And then I said, "May I ask if you are kind?"

"No. I'm not. I was once—when I was younger. Life has made me hard. I ought to be kinder. Perhaps one day I shall be. What do you think?"

I didn't know what to say, and so I remained silent.

"Please speak, Miss Eyre! Won't you tell me something about yourself?"

"I'll gladly speak. But I don't know what interests you. If you ask me questions, I'll answer them."

Mr. Rochester wanted to speak about himself. He said, "You'll find, Miss Eyre, that I have plenty of faults. My past has been shameful. When I was twenty-one, I made a great mistake—but that was not my fault. I took the wrong path then. I haven't found the right path yet. Perhaps I shall find it someday. Who can tell?"

When the clock struck nine, I got up. "I must go now, sir."

"Don't go yet! Wait a minute! Adele has just gone to put on her new dress. She's coming back now. Wait and see her!"

Adele came dancing into the room. "Isn't my new dress lovely?" she said. "And look at my new shoes! And my stockings!"

I smiled at the child. Mr. Rochester's face hardened. "Someday, I'll tell you her story," he said. "Good night."

Mr. Rochester told me Adele's story one afternoon while we were in the garden. Adele was the daughter of a French dancer whom he had loved. But the dancer had loved a musician. She had run away with him and left her child Adele behind. Mr. Rochester had pitied the child and had made himself Adele's guardian.

Mr. Rochester trusted me. When he saw me, he spoke kindly to me. In the evenings he invited me to sit with him. I spoke but little. I enjoyed listening to him. He had traveled much, and his conversation was very interesting. Those were happy evenings. How long could such happiness last?

I was asking myself that question one night. I was in bed but I couldn't sleep. I was thinking, "Mr. Rochester will go away soon—perhaps tomorrow. He never stays in Thornfield long, so Mrs. Fairfax says. When will he come back again? Will he ever come back again?" I was troubled, and my thoughts were sad.

The clock struck two and I heard a noise outside my door. I sat up in bed. My heart was beating fast. I was frightened. I asked in a trembling voice, "Who's there?" Nobody answered. "It must be the dog, Pilot," I said to myself. I tried to sleep. Then I heard a strange laugh outside my door. It was that wild, inhuman laugh that I had heard before. I heard footsteps. Somebody was walking along the passage on the top floor. A door was opened and shut. By whom? Was it Grace Poole?

"I must go and tell Mrs. Fairfax," I thought. And at once I jumped out of bed. I opened the door. The air in the passage was full of smoke! Something was burning! I rushed along the passage. Mr. Rochester's door was open. Clouds of smoke were coming from his room. The bed was on fire! Mr. Rochester lay there, still asleep!

I shook him, and I cried, "Wake up! Wake up!" But the smoke had made him senseless. I couldn't awaken him. I rushed to his washbasin and jug. Luckily they were full of water. I poured the water

over him. I rushed to my room. I took my own jug of water and used it to put out the fire. Mr. Rochester awoke.

"What's the matter?"

"A fire! There has been a fire!" I said, breathlessly. "Please get up!"

He got up. I fetched a candle. He looked around the room and at the bed, which was still smoking.

"Shall I call Mrs. Fairfax?" I asked him.

"No. Let her sleep!" He thought for a moment, and then he said to me, "Sit here quietly. I have to go upstairs."

He took the candle and went to the floor above. I sat there in the darkness, waiting. After a long time he came back. He looked pale and very sad.

"Now I understand," he said. Then he asked me, "Did you see anybody in the passage?"

"No, sir."

"Did you hear anyone?"

"I heard a laugh—a strange laugh. I think it was Grace Poole. She laughs like that."

"Ah, yes! Grace Poole. It was Grace Poole." Then he said to me, "Tell nobody what has happened. Nobody! You understand?"

I nodded and said, "Good night, sir!"

"Don't go yet! I must thank you. You've saved my life. Shake hands with me before you go."

I held out my hand to him.

"How can I thank you?" he asked.

"There is no need of thanks," I said. "Good night!"

"Don't go!"

"I'm cold, sir."

"Good night!" he said. "My dear rescuer, good night!"

I went back to bed, but I couldn't sleep. I lay there, restless and excited, till daylight came.

I didn't see Mr. Rochester the next morning. But I saw the servants, who were busy in his room. Grace Poole was among them. She was sewing. She was making new curtains for the bed.

"Good morning, miss!" she said to me, just as calmly as could be.

"Good morning, Grace!" I said. I then asked her, "What has happened here?"

"The master was reading in bed last night. He fell asleep. The candle set fire to the bed-curtains. But he woke up in time, and he put the fire out."

"Strange!" I said. "Did he wake anybody?"

"The servants' rooms are far from his. The servants heard nothing. Mrs. Fairfax always sleeps heavily, and she didn't hear anything. Perhaps you heard something, miss! Your room is close to Mr. Rochester's."

"Yes," I said, and I looked her straight in the eyes. "I heard a strange laugh."

Grace Poole calmly threaded her needle. Then she said, "A strange laugh! You were dreaming!"

"No, I wasn't dreaming."

"Have you told the master?"

"I haven't seen him this morning."

"Did you open your door?"

"No," I said, "I always lock my door when I go to bed."

"You are wise," she said. "You should always lock your door at night."

I went away. All morning I kept asking myself, "Did Grace Poole set fire to Mr. Rochester's bed? Why didn't Mr. Rochester send her away at once? He knew what she had done. He was a proud, strong man, and yet . . . Was he afraid of Grace Poole? Why?"

I waited impatiently for the evening. I wanted to ask Mr. Rochester many questions. Early in the evening a servant came to me. "Ah!" I thought, "Now I shall see Mr. Rochester." But she said, "Tea is ready, ma'am, in Mrs. Fairfax's room."

Mrs. Fairfax looked at me and said, "You look pale, Jane. You ate almost nothing at dinnertime. Are you well?"

"Oh, yes! I'm quite well," I answered.

Then Mrs. Fairfax said, "Mr. Rochester has a nice day for his journey."

"Journey! Has Mr. Rochester gone away?"

"Yes, he went away soon after breakfast."

"Is he going far?"

"He's gone to Mr. Eshton's house—the Leas—about ten miles away."

"And when will he come back?"

"Oh, he'll stay there for a week at least. They are having a party there. Everyone likes Mr. Rochester—especially the ladies."

"Are there any ladies at the Leas?"

"Oh, yes! There are Mrs. Eshton and her two daughters, who are very pretty girls. And there are Blanche and Mary Ingram, who are really beautiful. People say that Blanche Ingram is the most beautiful woman in the country."

"What does she look like?"

"She's tall, with big black eyes and long black curls. She has a fine voice, too. At Christmas, when we had a party here, she sang many songs with Mr. Rochester."

"Can Mr. Rochester sing well?"

"Oh, yes! They sang beautifully together."

"Is Blanche Ingram married?"

"No. Not yet. Neither she nor her sister has much money. Blanche will not marry till she can find a rich husband. She is hoping to marry Mr. Rochester, people say."

How sad I was when I heard this! How heavy my heart was!

Afterward, when I was in my room, I was angry with myself. "How foolish you are, Jane Eyre!" I said to myself. "How can Mr. Rochester like you? You are nothing but a poor governess. You are foolish and you are ugly. Blanche is beautiful. She is a lady. You are nothing—less than nothing!"

6 Guests in the House

After two weeks, Mrs. Fairfax received a letter from Mr. Rochester. We were having breakfast when the letter came. Mrs. Fairfax read the letter. I went on with my breakfast. But my hand shook so much that I spilled my tea.

Mrs. Fairfax looked up from her letter and said, "Mr. Rochester will be here in three days. He is bringing a lot of friends with him. I have to get the rooms ready." Mrs. Fairfax finished her breakfast in a hurry and started at once on her work.

In three days the house was ready. The washing, the brushing, the polishing, and the dusting were all finished. The house shone with cleanliness. Mrs. Fairfax was satisfied.

Mrs. Fairfax put on her best black silk dress and her gold watch. It was her duty to receive the guests, and to show them to their rooms. Then, in the afternoon, we heard the sound of horses and carriages. We looked out of the window. Four riders were coming. Behind them were two carriages. Two of the riders were young gentlemen. Then there was Mr. Rochester. Beside him rode a very beautiful young lady.

"Miss Blanche!" exclaimed Mrs. Fairfax.

She hurried downstairs. The hall was filled with the sound of voices. I listened, trying to catch Mr. Rochester's voice. Adele wanted to go downstairs to the company. I kept her with me. "When Mr. Rochester sends for you, you may go," I told her.

The evening passed. Mr. Rochester didn't send for us. There was music in the living room after dinner. Neither Adele nor I was invited.

The next day Mrs. Fairfax said, "Mr. Rochester wants Adele to meet the ladies after dinner tonight. And he would like you to be there."

"Oh! I can't," I cried. "I'm not used to fine company. Will you be there, Mrs. Fairfax?" I asked her.

"No. I have asked Mr. Rochester to excuse me." She continued, "I know how you feel, my dear. Go to the living room before they finish their dinner. Sit in a quiet corner. When the ladies come in, they won't notice you. Let Mr. Rochester see you there. After that, get up and leave as soon as you can. They won't see you."

That evening I put on my best dress. It was silver-gray in color. I had bought it for Miss Temple's wedding, and I had never worn it since then.

Adele and I sat in a corner of the empty living room. A bright fire was burning. A lot of candles were burning on the tables. There were flowers everywhere. Soon the ladies came in from the dining room. I rose when they entered. Adele went up to them and greeted them in French. Then she sat down on a couch between Amy and Louisa Eshton.

I sat in my corner, half-hidden by the window curtain. I had some sewing in my hand. I studied the ladies with interest. Blanche Ingram interested me most of all. Mrs. Fairfax had spoken the truth—she was very beautiful.

The gentlemen now came in. Mr. Rochester was the last of all. I picked up my sewing, and I tried to sew. But my eyes were drawn to his face. No, he was not handsome. But what an interesting face! How dear it was—to me. I watched him as he moved among his guests. He was smiling.

Coffee was brought in.

Blanche Ingram came up to Mr. Rochester. They were not far from me. I could hear what they were saying.

"Mr. Rochester," said Blanche Ingram, "where did you find that little thing?" and she pointed to Adele.

"In Paris."

"Why don't you send her to school?"

"I can't afford to do that. Schools are expensive, you know."

"You have a governess for her. I saw her when I

came in. There she is—behind that window curtain. Surely the governess costs you more than a school?"

"I haven't thought about that."

"When we were children," Blanche went on, "we had governesses—at least half a dozen of them, didn't we, Mama?" She turned to her mother, and then continued, without waiting for an answer, "How we hated them! They never stayed long with us—did they, Mama?"

"Don't talk about governesses!" said Lady Ingram. "They're all stupid!"

Mary Ingram whispered in her ear, "Be careful! The governess can hear you!"

"Let her hear!" said Lady Ingram. "She looks as dull as the rest of them."

"Let us move on to something interesting," said Blanche. "Mr. Rochester, will you sing for us?"

"If you wish, certainly," he replied.

"I will play for you," Blanche said.

"Now," I thought, "I can leave. Nobody will notice me now." But the singing was so beautiful that I stayed to listen. When Mr. Rochester had finished, I crept out through a side door.

In the hall, I noticed that my shoelace was untied. I bent down to tie it. While I was tying it, I heard the living room door open. Someone came out. I stood up—and found Mr. Rochester in front of me!

"Well, Miss Eyre, how are you?" he asked.

"I am very well, sir."

"Why didn't you speak to me in the living room?"

"I . . . I didn't want to trouble you."

"What have you been doing while I have been away?"

"Teaching Adele."

"You look pale. What is the matter?"

"Nothing. Nothing at all, sir."

"Come back to the living room. You're leaving too early."

"I'm tired, sir."

He looked at me. Then he said, "And you're unhappy. Why? Won't you tell me?"

"No, sir. I'm not unhappy."

Tears came into my eyes as I spoke. I turned my head away quickly.

"Tonight I shall excuse you. But I want you in the living room every evening while my guests are here. Go now! Good night," he said, and his voice was very gentle.

Thornfield Hall was a merry place while the guests were there. The house was full of life. In fine weather, the guests went outdoors—in the garden or the park. In wet weather, the guests stayed indoors—reading, playing cards, playing the piano, and talking.

One wet afternoon Mr. Rochester had to go to Millcote. While he was away, a gentleman arrived— a stranger. He was, he said, an old friend of Mr. Rochester. He had come from the West Indies where he had first met Mr. Rochester. He said his name was Richard Mason. He sat with the guests near the fire, waiting for Mr. Rochester's return.

That evening as the guests were having supper in the dining room, I noticed it had stopped raining. I stepped outside for some fresh air. Just then Mr. Rochester returned home.

"A stranger is waiting to see you," I told him. "He has come from the West Indies—from Jamaica. His name is Richard Mason."

"Mason!" Mr. Rochester's face suddenly became white. "Did you say Mason?" he asked.

"Are you ill, sir?" I asked.

"Oh, Jane!" he cried. "What shall I do now?"

"Can I help you, sir?"

"What are the guests doing, Jane?"

"They're having supper—talking and laughing."

"All of them?"

"Yes."

"Mason as well?"

"Oh, yes!"

Mr. Rochester took my hand, and said, very seriously, "Jane, if all these people turned against me, would you remain with me?"

"I would, sir."

"If all the world were against me, would you remain my friend?"

"I would, sir. I would never leave a friend who needed me."

"Thank you, Jane," Mr. Rochester said quietly. "Now go into the dining room and ask Mason to come here. Don't let the others hear you!"

I did what he asked.

Late that night, I heard Mr. Rochester's voice in the passage outside my room. He was talking to Mason, and his voice was cheerful. "This is your room, Mason. Sleep well! Good night!"

"All is well," I thought, and I fell asleep at once.

7 Strange Sounds in the Night

The moon was full that night. Its brightness awakened me. I was restless. Then suddenly, I heard a fearful scream. My heart beat fast. What was it? Who was it? I listened, trembling.

In the room above mine, somebody was fighting for his life. "Help! Help! She's killing me! Rochester! Help!"

Someone ran along the passage. Something fell heavily in the room above. Then there was silence.

I dressed quickly and left my room. The passage was full of people. "What's the matter?" they were asking. "What has happened? Have thieves broken in? Where's Rochester?"

Then I heard Mr. Rochester's voice: "Here I am! I'm coming. Be calm, all of you!" Mr. Rochester was hurrying down from the top floor.

"It's nothing," he said. "Nothing at all. Please go back to your beds. A servant has had a bad dream. That's all."

The ladies and gentlemen went back to their beds. I returned to my room but I didn't get into bed. I sat there by the window, waiting. "Mr. Rochester will need help," I thought. "I must be ready when he comes." I sat there for a long time.

The house was silent and still.

Somebody knocked softly on my door.

"Jane!"

"Yes, sir."

"Please come!"

Mr. Rochester stood outside. "I need your help, Jane," he said in a low voice. "Come with me . . . quietly!"

We walked softly along the long passage and upstairs to the top floor. Mr. Rochester took a key from his pocket and unlocked a door.

"You don't feel ill when you see blood, do you?" he asked.

"I don't know . . . I don't think so."

We went inside the room. Mr. Rochester walked across it toward another door. He unlocked that door also and went inside. I heard again that strange, inhuman laugh. Was Grace Poole in there?

Mr. Rochester came back. "Here, Jane," he said and pointed. Then I saw an armchair beside a large bed. Richard Mason was half-sitting, half-lying in it. His left arm was hanging down. His shirt sleeve was red with blood. Blood was also running from his arm to the floor. Already, there was a pool of blood on the floor.

"Hold the candle!" ordered Mr. Rochester.

I obeyed. He opened Mason's shirt and began washing his shoulder and arm. Mason opened his eyes.

"Is it bad?" he asked.

"Oh, no! It's nothing," Mr. Rochester said. "You'll be all right soon. You'll be able to leave in the morning. You'll soon be well again."

Mr. Rochester turned to me. "I'm going to fetch the doctor, Jane. You must stay here till I come back. Give him some water to drink. Wash his arm with clean water. But don't speak to him!"

Then he said to Mason, "You must be quiet. You mustn't say a word to her. If you get excited, you may die. Keep silent! If you don't, you'll be sorry!"

With that, Mr. Rochester left the room and locked the door behind him.

That was a fearful night for me. I was locked in with a sick man—perhaps a dying man. And who was in that next room? Sometimes I heard that strange, inhuman laugh. Sometimes I heard other strange sounds—sounds that a wild animal makes. Who was there? Grace Poole? A wild animal? Who? These were questions that I was asking myself. And there were other questions, too. Why mustn't I speak to Mason? Why mustn't Mason speak to me? What was Mason's secret?

The candle went out. I sat there in the darkness. I was filled with fear and sadness.

At last, the dawn came and the darkness ended. I heard a dog bark in the garden below. Mr. Rochester had come back! How thankful I was!

Mr. Rochester came in with the doctor.

"Now, Dr. Carter," he said, "you must work quickly. In half an hour he must leave." To Mason, he said, "How are you feeling now?"

"She's killed me this time. I'm dying."

"Nonsense! You've lost a little blood, that's all. Dr. Carter, tell him what you think!"

Dr. Carter examined the man's shoulder and arm.

"You're right, Mr. Rochester," he said. "It's nothing serious. There's no danger." Suddenly he cried, "What's this? This wound wasn't made by a knife! This wound was made by teeth!"

"She bit me," Mason said. "Rochester took the knife from her, and then she attacked me like a tigress!"

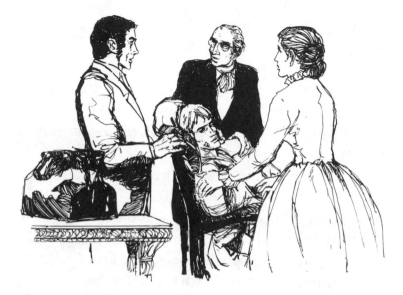

"I told you," Mr. Rochester said, "I told you! Why did you go in there alone? Why didn't you wait for me? Hurry, Dr. Carter!"

I trembled. Mr. Rochester turned to me and said, "Jane, go downstairs to my bedroom and bring me a clean shirt. Then go into Mason's room and get his coat." I obeyed. Very soon the wounded man was able to leave. He walked downstairs with the help of Mr. Rochester and Dr. Carter. They put him into the carriage which was waiting outside.

"Look after him well!" Mr. Rochester said to the doctor.

"Take care of her!" cried Mason.

"I've always taken care of her. And I always will," said Rochester.

The carriage drove away.

Mr. Rochester watched it leave. He gave a great sigh and said, "Jane, let us walk in the garden. I need fresh air."

It was a lovely spring morning. The sun was just rising. The garden was filled with flowers of all colors. The birds were singing. Mr. Rochester picked a rose and handed it to me.

"You look very pale, Jane. Were you afraid?"

"I was afraid of someone in the next room."

"But I had locked the door. You were safe."

"Is Grace Poole going to stay here, sir?"

"Yes. But don't worry about her."

"Your life is in danger while she is here."

"Never mind! I can take care of myself." His voice became very serious and he said, "Jane, there is something that I must tell you. Sit down beside me. Listen to me. When I was a young man, I made a bad mistake—a serious mistake. That mistake has ruined my life. I became very unhappy. I thought that if I could run away from that mistake, I would forget. And so I traveled here and there. I spent money freely. I lived wildly."

He sighed, fell silent, and then continued. "Jane, I was trying to run away from myself. No man can do that. My mistake followed me wherever I went. At last I met a stranger. With her I felt happy. I began to feel—as I did before my mistake—young and good. If that stranger will stay with me, I shall be a better man, I'm sure. I shall leave my life of false pleasure. I shall lead a really good life. Shall I ask that stranger to stay with me, Jane? Tell me what you think."

"Oh, sir," I answered, "only God can help us to lead a good life. We must trust in God."

There was a long silence before he spoke again. Now his voice was hard and cruel.

"I'm fond of Blanche Ingram. If I married her, shall I be a better man? What do you think, Jane?"

I didn't answer. I was filled with a great sadness. I couldn't say a word.

He got up and walked back to the house.

That afternoon a stranger came to see me. It was a servant from Gateshead—the coachman who had married Bessie.

"How is Bessie?" I asked him.

"She's very well, thank you, miss," he replied.

"And how is Mrs. Reed and her family?"

"Ah! I'm afraid I have some sad news for you," he said. He stopped a moment and then added, "Mr. John died last week."

"Mr. John!" I exclaimed.

"Yes. He lived a wild life and had bad companions. He spent his money like water. He was in prison twice for debt. His mother helped him, of course. But he spent all her money as well. In the end she refused to help him. She had to refuse.

She had hardly any money left. Then, a week ago, Mr. John killed himself."

This was sad news. But it was not all. The coachman went on, "Mrs. Reed fell ill when she heard of John's death. For three days she couldn't speak. When she was able to speak again, she said to Bessie, 'Fetch Jane Eyre. I have something to say to her.' Can you come back with me tomorrow?"

"Yes," I answered.

I went to look for Mr. Rochester. I found him with his guests. Miss Ingram was standing close beside him.

"May I speak to you for a moment, sir?" I asked him.

Mr. Rochester followed me out of the room.

"Well, Jane," he said, "what is the matter?"

I explained the situation to him.

"Promise me you will come back in a week's time," he said.

"I can't promise that, sir. I may have to stay with her."

"But you will come back? You won't stay with her long? Promise me that, Jane!"

"I'll come back when all is well. But there is something else I must say. You have told me that you will marry soon. If you do that, I think you should send Adele away to school."

"Ah! I see. Perhaps you are right. And you? What shall I do about you?"

"I shall have to look for work somewhere else. I shall advertise."

"You will advertise!" he exclaimed, looking very angry. But his face quickly became kind again and he said, "Promise me that you won't advertise. I'll find work for you, I promise."

"Very well, sir. I won't advertise. But you must assure me that Adele and I will be out of the house when your bride arrives."

"I promise. When are you leaving?"

"Tomorrow, sir. Very early."

"Then I must say good-bye."

"Good-bye, sir!" I said.

The dinner bell rang, and Mr. Rochester walked quickly away.

8 Gateshead Revisited

I left Thornfield early in the morning. I arrived at Gateshead late in the afternoon. First of all, I went to see Bessie. She looked well and happy. I remembered how I had left the house nine years ago. I had been angry then, alone and helpless. Now I felt only a great sadness.

We went into the living room. It looked just the same. Mrs. Reed's two daughters both greeted me politely but coldly. I left them at once and went to see their mother.

I went into Mrs. Reed's bedroom. Standing beside her bed, I bent down and kissed her. I felt better when I had done that. We all feel better when we forget our anger and forgive.

"How are you, dear Aunt?" I asked her softly.

"Is it Jane Eyre?" she asked me, weakly.

I took her pale hand, and I held it for a moment. She took her hand away and turned her face to the wall. Tears came into my eyes.

"You sent for me, Aunt," I said quietly.

"Ah, yes! I have something to tell you," she said in a weak voice. She was silent for a long time. At last she asked, "Are you really Jane Eyre?"

"Yes, Aunt."

"Ah! The trouble I had with that child. How glad
I was when she went away. Why didn't she die in
Lowood!"

"Why did you hate her so?"

"I hated her mother. But my husband loved his
sister—and he loved her child. He loved Jane more
than his own children. Ah! Ah! My John's dead.

Poor, poor boy!" Mrs. Reed began to cry then. I had to pity her. Her heart was broken.

Bessie came near the bed. She gave Mrs. Reed some medicine that made her quiet. I left the room silently.

I waited for my aunt to send for me again. Ten days passed without a word from her. I went to see her again. She was lying very still, but she heard me come in.

"Who is that?" she asked in a very weak voice.

After I told her, she began to speak. She spoke slowly and stopped often, for she could hardly breathe.

"Is there anybody else here?"

"Nobody."

"Then I shall tell you something. I am dying. Go to my writing desk. Bring me the letter in the top drawer."

I obeyed her.

"Read it!"

I read:

Dear Mrs. Reed,

Will you kindly send me the address of my niece, Jane Eyre. I want her to come and live with me in Jamaica. I have neither wife nor children. I want Jane to be my daughter. When I die, I shall leave her all I have.

Yours faithfully,
John Eyre

I looked at the date of the letter. That letter was three years old!

"Why didn't you tell me before?" I asked.

"I hated you. I wanted to hurt you. I answered that letter. I told your uncle that you were dead."

"Never mind!" I said. "Never mind! Let us forget all this, dear Aunt!"

I bent down to kiss her, but she turned her face away. I took her hand. It was icy cold. She lay still. I sat beside her but she didn't speak again. She died that same night.

As soon as the funeral was over, I returned to Thornfield Hall. Everyone was pleased to see me. Little Adele was wild with joy. I felt glad to be coming home.

The next two weeks passed peacefully. Strangely, nobody spoke about Mr. Rochester's wedding. He never went to visit the Ingrams. He looked happier than before. And he spoke to me so kindly! Almost every evening I sat with him and Adele in the living room. I listened happily while he talked to me. I liked him more and more.

9 A Question of Marriage

One evening I was taking a walk in the garden. The air was warm and the garden smelled sweet. I sat down to watch the moon rise. How beautiful everything was! How peaceful!

Then Mr. Rochester came out into the garden.

"Jane, won't you take a little walk with me?" he said.

We walked together down the garden path. Then we sat down under a great tree at the other end of the garden.

"Yes," he said, "Thornfield is a pleasant place at this time of the year. Will you be sorry to leave it, Jane?"

"Must I leave it, sir?"

"I'm afraid you will want to."

"Then you are going to marry, sir?"

"Yes, Jane. I hope to marry in a month's time. I've already found work for you. A lady in Ireland whom I know well has five daughters. Would you like to be their governess?"

"Ireland is far away, sir," I answered sadly.

"Never mind! The work will be interesting. You will forget me there—I think."

"Oh, no! I shall never forget you. How can I?" I began to weep.

"Oh, sir! I love Thornfield. I love living here. Everyone is so kind to me—you, above all. How can I go away from Thornfield! How can I go away from you!"

"Why must you go away, Jane?"

"How can I stay here when your bride comes? I am poor. I am plain—I know that. But I am not without feelings. . . ." I was weeping all the time while I was speaking. At last I became calmer, and I said quietly, "Very well, sir. I shall go to Ireland."

"Will you marry me, Jane?"

I couldn't believe my ears. I didn't answer. I was so surprised that I couldn't speak!

"I love you, Jane. I love you—only you. And I shall love you forever."

I still couldn't speak. He continued, "Miss Ingram is nothing to me. I have never loved her. I wanted to make you jealous, Jane. Forgive me! And she—she never loved me. She loved only my money. Marry me, Jane!"

"Do you love me truly?"

"I do."

"Then I will marry you."

I promised to marry Mr. Rochester in a month's time. Mr. Rochester wanted to buy me rich clothes and jewels. I refused them all. At the same time, I wished I were not so poor. Then I remembered my uncle in Jamaica. "I shall write to him," I thought. "I'll tell him that I'm alive. I must also tell him that I am going to marry Mr. Rochester." I wrote to him at once.

The days passed very quickly. I taught Adele in the mornings. In the evenings I sat with Mr. Rochester in the living room. Ah, those were happy hours!

Two nights before the wedding, I was restless and excited. I couldn't sleep. I tossed and turned. I listened to the rain outside. Then I heard again that strange, inhuman laugh! At last I fell asleep.

I rose early on my wedding day. At seven o'clock the maid came in to help me dress. The carriage, with our luggage, was already at the door. After our wedding we would be leaving Thornfield for a time.

We hurried toward the little gray church. The sky was still red from the sunrise. I noticed two strangers in the churchyard. But Mr. Rochester didn't see them.

We entered the church. It was very peaceful inside. We walked together toward the clergyman who was standing in front of the altar. The service began at once. To me it was like a dream. Then suddenly someone shouted from the back of the church:

"Stop! This marriage can't go on."

One of the strangers came forward. "Mr. Rochester cannot marry this woman," he said. "His wife is still living."

I looked at Mr. Rochester. His face was stony. His eyes flashed lightning.

"Who are you?" he asked the stranger.

"I'm a lawyer. My name is Briggs."

"And you say that I have a wife?"

"Yes," said the lawyer. He took a piece of paper from his pocket.

"Listen to this!" He began to read from the paper:

Edward Rochester of Thornfield Hall married my sister in Jamaica fifteen years ago. I have a copy of the marriage certificate.

Richard Mason

"You say that my wife is still living?"

"She was living three months ago. This gentleman saw her then." The lawyer pointed to the second stranger. "Come forward, Mr. Mason!" he said.

Richard Mason came forward. Mr. Rochester raised his arm. He was ready to strike Mason. Mason stepped back with a cry of fear.

"Sir!" said the clergyman to Mr. Rochester. "Remember you are in a church." Then he asked Mason, "Is this man's wife still living?"

"She's living in Thornfield Hall. I saw her there last April."

"Living in Thornfield!" exclaimed the clergyman. "Are you sure? I've been living near Thornfield all my life and I've never heard of Mrs. Rochester."

"You shall see her!" said Mr. Rochester. "But first I shall tell you the whole story."

"It is true that I have a wife," Mr. Rochester began. "It is true that she is living in Thornfield. But she is mad! Her mother was the same—a madwoman and a heavy drinker!" Mr. Rochester stopped a moment. Then he continued, "It was my father's fault. He wanted me to marry a rich woman. He sent me to Jamaica to stay with the Masons—old friends of his. He did not tell me that there was madness in that family. He told me only that Bertha was the most beautiful woman in Jamaica. He told me the truth about that. She was beautiful. We got married. Shortly afterward she began to drink heavily. Soon she became mad. I brought Bertha to Thornfield. I hired Grace Poole to look after her. Carter, the doctor, knows the secret, too. Mrs. Fairfax knew something—but not all. This young woman knew nothing. But come with me, gentlemen, and you shall see Mrs. Rochester."

I walked beside Mr. Rochester. The three gentlemen followed.

The carriage was still standing at the door. "Take that away!" Mr. Rochester ordered. "We have no need of that now!"

Mrs. Fairfax and the servants were standing at the door to welcome the bride and the bridegroom. "Away!" said Mr. Rochester roughly.

He hurried to the third floor. He walked to the door of the room where Mason had lain. He unlocked the second door. We all entered Grace Poole's room.

The room had no window. The light came from the fire and a lamp. Grace Poole was bending over the fire, cooking. In a dark corner, something was moving. We looked. Was it a human being—or an animal? Like an animal, it was creeping over the floor. Like an animal, it was growling. Its face was hidden under long black hair.

"How is she today, Grace?" Mr. Rochester asked.

"About the same. Neither better nor worse."

The madwoman stood up straight.

"Be careful, sir! She has seen you!" cried Grace
Poole.

The madwoman growled. She pushed her hair
away from her face and looked wildly at us.

"Take care!" cried Grace Poole. "She's danger-
ous!"

The three gentlemen ran toward the door. Mr.
Rochester pushed me behind him. Just in time!
The madwoman sprang at him. She held him by

the throat. She bit his cheek. Mr. Rochester didn't strike her. He caught her arms and pushed her into a chair. He held her there while Grace Poole tied her to the chair with a rope. Mr. Rochester turned then to the three gentlemen and said, "That is my wife! And this young woman," he said pointing to me, "is the one I wished to marry today. You see the difference! Can you blame me, gentlemen?"

Nobody spoke. We all left the room except Mr. Rochester, who stayed behind to speak to Grace Poole. As we went downstairs, the lawyer said to me, "I shall tell your uncle of this."

"My uncle? Do you know him?"

"Mr. Mason knows him well. Your uncle told Mr. Mason about your letter. Then Mason told him about Rochester's wife—Mason's sister. Your uncle sent Mason here to stop your marriage. Your uncle is now very ill. If he were not, I should take you back to Jamaica with me. I shall write to you about your uncle when I get back to Jamaica. Be brave, Miss Eyre! Be patient!"

"Come! Let us go!" said Mason. The three gentlemen left the house.

I went up to my room. My heart was very heavy, but I couldn't cry. I took off my wedding dress. Then I sat down and buried my head in my arms. I was too sad for tears! I had lost all my hope, all feeling of happiness.

10 A Sad Journey

I spent the rest of the day alone in my room. "What am I going to do now?" I asked myself. The answer came at once. I must leave Thornfield. I must go away at once. Then I thought, "How can I go away? I love this place. I love its master!" For a long time, I couldn't decide.

At midnight I got up. I put a few clothes together in a bundle. I took my purse. I crept softly out of my room. Outside Mr. Rochester's door I stopped a moment. I heard his footsteps. He was walking up and down. Probably he was too troubled to sleep. He was suffering. He needed me. But I went on my way. In the kitchen I drank some water and ate some bread. Then I left the house.

I walked on and on—away from Millcote. The morning came—and I still walked on. I was crying all the time. Then I felt so weak that I fell to the ground. I got up again. But I was too weak to go on. As I was sitting on a stone, a coach came by. I showed the driver the money in my purse. "Take me as far as you can!" I told him.

I traveled in that coach till evening. I got out and stood there in the road, alone! Yes, I was alone and penniless. I had left my bundle of clothes in the coach. I had nothing! I looked at the signpost. The nearest town was ten miles away. I was too tired to walk. I picked some wild fruit to eat. I lay down on the grass and fell asleep.

The next day I walked on in the direction of the town. I felt weak and ill. Then I heard the sound of church bells, and soon I came to a village. I went into a baker's shop—but I had no money for bread. I asked the woman there, "Please, may I sit down for a minute?" After I had rested a little, I asked again, "Is there a dressmaker in the village?"

"Yes. There are two or three. We don't need a dressmaker here."

"Do you know anybody who needs a servant?"

"No, I don't."

I took out my handkerchief and showed it to her. "Will you give me a little bread for this?" I begged.

"No! I sell bread for money, not for a hand-kerchief!"

"She thinks I am a thief!" I thought. Well, I couldn't blame her!

I went on my way till I came to a wood. I lay down there but I couldn't sleep. The ground was wet. It began to rain. I wanted to die!

The next day, I walked till evening. Then I couldn't go on. I felt so ill! At that moment I saw a white gate. I opened it and walked to a window where a light was shining. I looked in. An old woman—a servant—was sewing at the table. Two young ladies were sitting by the fire. They were reading. I felt that they might help me, so I went to the door and knocked.

"What do you want?"

"May I speak to the young ladies?" I begged weakly.

"Who are you? Where do you come from?"

"I'm a stranger."

"Why have you come here?"

"Can you give me a piece of bread and a place to sleep?"

"You can't stay here. Here, take this and go away!" She gave me a penny, shut the door, and locked it.

I sank to the ground. I wept. "Oh, God! Let me die," I cried.

"We must all die—but you are young," a voice said.

I looked up. A tall gentleman stood there. He was knocking on the door. "Hannah! Hannah! Let me in!" he cried.

"Is it you, Mr. St. John?"

Hannah opened the door. "You're wet through, Mr. St. John!" she exclaimed. She saw me then and she cried, "Get up! Go away!"

"No, Hannah!" said St. John. "She's coming inside with me."

He helped me to get up and to walk into the kitchen. I fell into a chair. I was too weak to stand. One of the young ladies brought me some milk. I drank it right away. Then she gave me some bread.

St. John asked me, "What is your name?"

"My name is Jane . . . Elliott," I answered weakly.

"Where do you live? Have you any friends? Is there anybody who can help you?"

I shook my head. I could hardly speak. I felt so tired and so ill! St. John looked at me silently for a time and then said, "Hannah! Get a bed ready!"

They helped me upstairs. Soon I was in a warm bed. I thanked God with all my heart and fell into a deep sleep.

For three days I lay there, very ill. Hannah looked after me. The two young ladies came to sit with me. St. John came to see me only once.

"She is very weak," he said. "But she doesn't need a doctor. She'll be better after a rest."

On the fourth day I felt stronger. I could speak and sit up in bed. I had an appetite. I was able to dress myself, and I went downstairs.

Hannah was cooking in the kitchen when I went in. She smiled at me and said kindly, "Sit there by the fire!" She went on with her work. After a time she asked me, "You aren't really a beggar, are you?"

"No! I'm no beggar," I answered.

"But you have no money and no home. . . ."

"I am a lady—as your mistresses are." Then I asked her, "What is the name of the family here?"

"Rivers. The old father died only three weeks ago."

"And the mother?"

"She died many years ago. I've looked after the home and the children for many years."

"Hannah! You're an honest and faithful servant. But you were unkind to me when I first came here. You refused to give me a piece of bread. That was wrong, Hannah! We must always help the poor—surely you know that!"

"Mr. St. John has often said that to me." After a moment she said, "Yes, I was wrong."

"Well, let us shake hands!" We shook hands and we both smiled. Hannah was my friend now.

While she worked, Hannah told me about the Rivers family. The young ladies were governesses. They were now at home because their father had died. Their brother, St. John, was a clergyman. He lived and worked in Morton, a few miles away.

While Hannah was talking, St. John and his sisters came in.

"Why are you sitting here in the kitchen? Come into the living room. It's more comfortable there," said Diana.

We had our tea in the living room. I ate hungrily. St. John looked up from his book, and said, "You're very hungry!"

"Yes," I said. Then I added, "I'm a great trouble to you, I'm afraid."

"Won't you tell us the addresses of your friends? We can write to them. We can tell them you are safe."

"That is quite impossible."

"Have you any family?" asked St. John.

"None."

"And you're not married?"

"No," I answered, and the tears came into my eyes.

"Don't ask her any more questions!" cried Mary.

But St. John went on, "Where did you live before you came here?"

"I can't tell you that."

"But we can't help you unless you tell us something about yourself."

I looked him straight in the face and said, "Mr. St. John, you and your sisters have been very kind to me. You have saved my life. And so I will tell you this: I am an orphan. I was brought up in Lowood School. I left it and became a governess. I had to leave Th . . . the place where I was living. Don't blame me for that! It wasn't my fault. I had only a little money with me and a few clothes. Foolishly, I left my clothes in a coach. Then I had nothing. I just walked on and on till you found me and took me into your home."

"Don't ask her anything else, St. John," cried Diana. "Can't you see how weak she is? Come nearer to the fire, Miss Elliott." Miss Elliott! That was my name now. I had forgotten it!

"Your name is Jane Elliott, isn't it?" St. John asked me.

"Yes."

"Would you like to stay here with us?"

"Oh, yes—till I can find work. Please let me stay with you. I don't want to be homeless again!"

"You shall stay here!" Diana said.

"Yes, you shall!" Mary repeated.

"You see, my sisters want to keep you here. And I shall try to find some work for you," St. John said.

I sat by the fire a little longer. Then I went to bed, for I still felt weak and tired.

The next day I felt stronger. With each passing day my health improved. Soon I was able to go for long walks with Mary and Diana. I liked the two young women more and more. We became close friends for we shared the same sort of feelings and ideas. We read together. Diana taught me German, and I taught Mary drawing. The time passed pleasantly. We seldom saw St. John. He seldom came to see us. He was very busy in Morton. Besides his work in the church, he visited the poor and the sick. He did this in good weather and bad. He never failed in his duty.

A month passed. Diana and Mary had to return to their work in the south of England. "What shall I do after they have gone?" I kept asking myself. I became more and more worried.

One morning, when St. John was in the house, I went up to him. "May I ask you if you have found any work for me?"

"Yes. I found something a week or two ago. But you and my sisters were very happy together, and so I waited."

"What work have you found for me?"

"Hard work, I'm afraid," he said, "but good work. Work is always good when it helps others. Some time ago I started a school for the poor boys in Morton. Now I shall start a school for the girls. I have already rented a building, and a small house for the schoolmistress. Will you be the school-mistress?"

"Mr. St. John," I answered, "I thank you with all my heart. I shall be very glad to work in your school."

My answer pleased St. John, and he smiled.

Diana and Mary grew sadder each day. They were sorry they had to leave home. They had some sad news, too. Their Uncle John had died.

"We never knew him well because he always lived abroad," Diana told me. "He was a rich man and he has left all his money to his niece. That's a pity. If we had more money, we should be able to stay at home. Ah, well. Never mind."

The next day the two sisters left. I left at the same time. I began my work as schoolmistress in the village of Morton.

The work was hard at first. In the evenings, I was often tired and glad to be alone. I used to read or draw then. At night, however, I had strange, unhappy dreams about Mr. Rochester. One evening, while I was drawing, St. John came to see me.

"How are you getting on?" he asked quite kindly. "Look! I've brought you a book to read."

I thanked him. While I was looking at the book, he looked at my drawing. Then he picked up a piece of paper that was beside my drawing. He studied it. He stared at me. He put the paper in his pocket and left soon after. I thought this very strange, but I soon forgot about it.

11 My Three Cousins

That night there was a snowstorm. The snow fell all through the next day. In the evening, it lay deep on the ground. I was very surprised when St. John came to see me again.

"What's the matter?" I asked. "Have you any bad news? Are your sisters well?"

"They are quite well," he answered.

"But why have you come out—on a night like this?"

"I've come," he said, "because I must tell you a story about a poor orphan. Her parents died when she was a baby. Her uncle took her into his home. After his death the child stayed there with her aunt, a woman called Mrs. Reed. She lived in a house called Gateshead."

"Mr. St. John!" I exclaimed. But he didn't stop.

"The orphan was sent to Lowood School. She became a teacher there. After that she became a governess in the house of Mr. Rochester—"

"Stop! Please stop!" I cried. But he continued with his story.

"Mr. Rochester asked this young woman to marry him. She promised. On the wedding day she learned a sad thing. Mr. Rochester already had a wife. That wife was living in Thornfield. She was a madwoman. The young woman ran away. Nobody knew where she had gone to. They haven't found her yet."

"How do you know all this?" I cried.

"I found out your name yesterday. It was on that piece of paper I took away with me. You had written it there without thinking. Look!" He held out the paper that he had put in his pocket. "I've had a letter from Mr. Briggs, the lawyer. He told me the story."

"Why?"

"He's looking for you."

"Why?"

"He wants to tell you that your uncle in Jamaica is dead. He has left you all his money—twenty thousand pounds. You are a rich woman now!"

I couldn't believe my ears! I! Rich!

But there was something that I didn't understand. "Why did Mr. Briggs write to you about me?" I asked. "Did Mr. Briggs know you? Is he a friend of yours? Tell me, please, I must know."

St. John then asked me, "Do you know my name?"

"Of course I do! Your name is St. John Rivers."

"My full name is St. John Eyre Rivers. My mother's name was Eyre," he explained. "She had two brothers. One of them married Miss Jane Reed of Gateshead—your mother. The other was John Eyre, a merchant of Jamaica. Mr. Briggs wrote to us some time ago. He told us of Uncle John's death. Perhaps you may remember that letter? Uncle John left all his money to his niece, Jane Eyre. Mr. Briggs asked me to find that niece, and I have found her!"

"So, your mother was my father's sister?"

"Yes."

"Your Uncle John was my Uncle John?"

"Yes."

"Then Diana and Mary and you are my cousins?"

"That's right."

"Oh! I am so glad!" I exclaimed. "I had nobody in the world—and now I have three cousins! How glad I am! How very glad I am!" My face was red with excitement. My heart was beating fast.

"Be calm, Miss Eyre! May I bring you a glass of water? You are too excited. You will be ill!"

"Oh, no. Mr. St. John, you must write to your sisters—my cousins. Tell them they must come home at once. Tell them they each have five thousand pounds!"

"I don't understand."

"Divide twenty thousand pounds by four, and we each have five thousand pounds."

"But it's your money!"

"It's our money!"

"And you, Miss Eyre, what about you? Will you stop working? Shall I have to close the school?"

"Oh, no. Certainly not."

For some time, my cousins refused to accept the money. In the end, they did, and I am glad they did.

We had a merry Christmas together—Diana, Mary, and I. St. John was never merry. He was always very serious. He was studying an Indian

language. He wanted to go to India as a missionary.

One afternoon, Diana and Mary were out. I was alone with St. John. "What are you doing, Jane?" he asked me suddenly.

"I'm studying German."

"I want you to learn Hindustani instead of German. In three months I shall go to India. I must know Hindustani well. If I can repeat my lessons with you, I shall learn faster. Will you help me, Jane?"

I couldn't refuse. I began to study Hindustani with St. John, but I didn't like it.

All this time, I had had no news of Mr. Rochester. I thought of him so often! I dreamed about him nearly every night. My dreams were sad and troubled, but I could not find any news of him.

I wrote to Mr. Briggs and asked him about Mr. Rochester. He wrote back saying that he had no news of him, either. I wrote to Mrs. Fairfax, but I received no answer to my letter. I didn't know what to do.

"You're looking ill," Diana said to me. "You need a holiday by the sea."

"She doesn't need a holiday," said St. John. "She needs a purpose in life. Her present life is aimless. We all need an aim in life. Without that, we can never be happy or well."

12 Mr. Rochester's Voice

St. John and I went on with our study of Hindustani. One evening, while we were studying, St. John said to me, "Jane, in six weeks, I shall leave for India. The boat sails on the 20th of June." He paused and then said, "Jane, come with me to India!"

"Oh, no!" I cried. "Don't ask me to do that! I can't. It's impossible!"

"It's quite possible," he said. "I have watched you for some time, Jane. You will make a good wife for a missionary. I've seen how you worked in the village school. I've seen how you help others. You can help girls and women in India. You can help me in my work there."

"Oh, no! I can't live in India. I can't leave England."

"Ah! You are thinking of Mr. Rochester. You don't want to leave him!"

I was silent. I didn't know what to say. He had spoken the truth. I didn't want to be far away from Mr. Rochester.

That night, when everyone was in bed, I lay sleepless. "Shall I go to India? Shall I be St. John's wife? I have no hope of being Mrs. Rochester. What shall I do? In India I can help others—that is true. But how can I leave Mr. Rochester? He needs me." These thoughts went through my mind again and again.

Suddenly I heard a voice cry, "Jane! Jane! Jane!" It was Mr. Rochester's voice. Where was he?

I ran outside, calling, "I'm coming. Wait for me! Oh, please wait." But Mr. Rochester was nowhere in the garden. I cried, "Where are you? Oh! Where are you? Speak to me!" There was no answer. I searched everywhere in the garden. No! He wasn't there. I went back into the house.

I went back upstairs to my room. I fell on my knees and I prayed. Then I lay down, waiting for the morning. I now knew what I must do.

At sunrise I got up and dressed. My thoughts were troubled, but I had decided what to do. I would return at once to Thornfield. Mr. Rochester

had called me. He needed me. He must be in great trouble.

At breakfast I said to Diana and Mary, "I have to go away—but I shall be absent only a few days. I must see a friend of mine. I'm afraid he is ill."

That morning I took the coach to Millcote. I left my bags at the inn and walked across the fields to Thornfield Hall.

My heart was beating fast. I came to the high wall of the garden. "Perhaps Mr. Rochester is walking there," I thought. "What shall I say to him? What will he say to me?" I walked on to the gate. I looked through it.

There was no Thornfield! There was only a black ruin! The Hall had been burnt to the ground!

What had happened? Where was Mr. Rochester? Was he alive or dead? And where was Mrs. Fairfax—and Adele? Were they living? Had everyone died in that fire? I went back to the inn at once. I sat down and ordered something to eat. When the innkeeper came, I asked him, "Do you know Thornfield Hall?"

"Oh, yes, ma'am! But it was burnt down last autumn. A fire broke out in the middle of the night. It was fearful! I saw it with my own eyes."

"And what caused the fire?"

"A madwoman, ma'am. She was Mr. Rochester's wife. She set fire to the house."

"Was Mr. Rochester there at that time?"

"He was, ma'am. And he acted very bravely. He was a real hero. He took all the servants out of the house. Then he went back to save his wife. She was on the roof, shouting and waving and screaming. I saw her myself. She was really mad, poor thing! Mr. Rochester climbed to the roof to save her. I heard him shout, 'Bertha! Bertha!' Then I heard her scream. She jumped from the roof. There she lay—"

"Dead? Was she dead?"

"All broken and dead, ma'am."

"Did anybody else die?"

"No."

"And Mr. Rochester?"

"Well, he's alive, that's true, but—"

"But what? What happened to him? Tell me!"

"He's now blind and has lost one hand."

"Oh! Tell me, where is he living now?"

"At Ferndean. That's a farmhouse about thirty miles away."

"Who is looking after him?"

"Two old servants. He won't have anybody else near him. He never goes out now. They say he's not doing very well."

"Have you a carriage?"

"A very nice one, ma'am."

"Get it ready at once! I must go to Ferndean."

We reached Ferndean late in the evening. A cold wind was blowing, and a light rain was falling.

There seemed to be no life inside the house. "Can he be here?" I asked myself.

I went up to the door and knocked. A servant opened it. She couldn't believe her eyes when she saw me.

"You! Miss Eyre! Is it you?"

I followed her into the kitchen. Just then a bell rang. "The master wants a glass of water and candles. He always asks for candles in the evening—although he's blind."

"I'll take them to him."

I went to the living room. Mr. Rochester was bending over the fire. His old dog, Pilot, lay beside him. The dog jumped up at once when I came in. It ran toward me. "Down, Pilot!" I said softly. I walked slowly and quietly toward Mr. Rochester.

"Give me the water!" he said, and held out his hand.

Pilot was jumping round me. "Down, Pilot!" I cried again.

Mr. Rochester heard me. "Who . . . who is there?" he asked. "Answer me! Speak!"

"It's Jane," I said. "I've come home." I put my hand in his.

"Jane! Yes, it's Jane—I know this little hand." And then he asked, "Is it true, Jane? You have come back to me?"

"It's true, sir."

"Oh, Jane! Oh, Jane! These hopeless months—without you! You won't leave me again, Jane?"

"Never, sir! I'll never leave you again." I added, "But it's your suppertime now. You must have something to eat."

Soon a meal was on the table. Mr. Rochester ate but little. But now and then he smiled. Some of the sadness left his face.

"Where have you been all these months, Jane?"

"I'll tell you the whole story tomorrow. It's late. I'm tired after my journey, and I must go to bed. I'll ask a servant to find me a place to sleep. Good night, sir!" I said.

"Good night, dear Jane!" he answered.

Early the next morning, I heard Mr. Rochester go downstairs. I heard his voice. "Is Miss Eyre up yet? Go and ask her if she wants anything. Ask her when she will come down."

I dressed and went downstairs. Mr. Rochester was in the living room. His face was full of sadness.

"It's a lovely morning, sir," I said to him, cheerfully. "We must go out for a walk." When he heard me, his face changed at once. The sadness disappeared. He smiled.

We spent the whole morning in the garden. There I told him my story.

"And this St. John," he said, "tell me more about him!"

"He's my cousin."

"Do you like him?"

"He's a very good man."

"How old is he?"

"He's twenty-nine."

"What does he look like?"

"He's tall and quite handsome."

"And clever?"

"Oh, very!"

Mr. Rochester was clearly jealous!

"Did St. John visit you often?"

"Every day—when I was teaching in his school."

"And when you were at home?"

"We studied together."

"Oh, and what did you study?"

"Hindustani. He was teaching me Hindustani."

"Why?"

"He wanted me to go to India with him."

"He wanted to marry you?"

"Yes. He asked me to marry him."

"And you refused?"

"Yes."

"Why?"

"He doesn't love me. And I certainly don't love him. He thought I would be a good wife for a missionary. He was wrong. I could never marry him."

"Is this true, Jane?"

"Every word!"

"Jane, will you marry me? I'm a poor, blind man now. But, will you marry me, Jane?"

"Gladly, sir!" I said. Later Mr. Rochester told me about a strange happening.

"A few days ago—last Monday night—Jane," he said, "I felt so sad, so hopeless! My Jane is dead, I thought. I shall never see her again. I wanted to die. I called you, 'Jane! Jane! Jane!' And I heard your voice answering me, my dear. Yes! I heard your voice. 'I'm coming. Wait for me!' you said. Can you believe that, Jane?"

"I can," I answered, "because I did hear you call me and I did say I was coming."

A few days later we were married. I wrote at once to tell my cousins. Diana and Mary were glad. St. John did not answer my letter at once, but later on he wrote to me from India, telling me about his work there.

Adele was in school at that time. I went to see her. Because she looked pale and thin and unhappy, I brought her home to live with us.

Mr. Rochester was blind for two years. Then one morning he said to me, "Jane! Jane! I can see something shining round your neck. What is it?"

"It's my gold chain."

"And are you wearing a pale blue dress?"

"Yes."

From that day his sight grew stronger. When our son was born, he was able to see him. That was indeed a happy day! I fell on my knees and I thanked the good God.